POINTS
of BALANCE

24 spiritual principles to empower your life

Dr Mansukh Patel
& Chris Barrington

 PUBLICATIONS

Published in the United Kingdom by
    Dru Publications
    Dru (UK), Nant Ffrancon, Bangor, North Wales, LL57 3LX
    Email: hello@druworldwide.com
    www.druworldwide.com

ISBN 978-1-873606-36-0

Printed in the United Kingdom by SS Media Ltd

Dru (UK) is a group of people committed to
providing the highest quality self help approaches
for optimising health and wellbeing. We are a team
of professionals from a wide range of backgrounds.
We help people to make more out of their lives by
teaching self-development methods drawn from many
different disciplines to integrate body, heart and mind
and to promote physical wellbeing, emotional balance,
successful relationships and personal fulfilment.

Dedication

To all those noble and courageous people who have
kept our humanity alive during the last century. These
are brave men and women such as Mahatma Gandhi,
Albert Einstein, Mother Teresa, Rabindranath Tagore
and Martin Luther King Jr.

Contents

Ancient yoga principles for modern living

There has never been a greater need for people to find an effective means to live at ease with their world and themselves, than there is today. World peace, more than ever before, needs our full and active participation.

Over the years many people have asked us what they can do to contribute to world peace. Our answer has always been to invite them to live peacefully. This is, of course, easier said than done because we each need clear directives and goals to achieve this aim.

This book is a collection of the principles that we have been living for the last twenty years. We believe that these principles hold many of the answers humanity is seeking.

Mansukh and I met at university during the mid '70s where we struck up a friendship that has lasted more than 30 years. Together we and a few friends created what is now Dru UK, with the intention of helping people find a sense of balance in their lives – physically, emotionally, mentally and spiritually.

Our driving force and inspiration came from Mansukh's parents, Chhaganbhai and Ecchaben Patel.

When I first met them at university they appeared on the surface much like any other Asian couple who had left their indigenous backgrounds in India and Kenya, to live in Britain during the late '60s. Very soon, however, it became apparent that these were two extraordinary human beings, unlike any others I had ever met.

In the midst of what must have been a very alien, fast moving world, they were able to live peacefully, seemingly unaffected by the hub-bub and chaos of modern western living. I began to notice that no matter what was happening around them, they always remained calm and content, at ease with their surroundings. I was intrigued. What was their secret?

Over the next few years they became our mentors. They taught us how to approach life with the utmost poise and balance, drawing on the wisdom of ages that they had accumulated throughout their lives. With their guidance, we were able to integrate this ancient wisdom known as the Controls and Directives, into a modern context and create a model for living peacefully in the 21st century.

What are the Controls and Directives?

In the ancient Indian treatise known as the *Srimad Bhagavatam** an extraordinary dialogue takes place between a warrior prince and his elite student in which the qualities needed in order to live a peaceful and fulfilling life are expounded. They are known as the Yamas and Niyamas.

Yamas are like the brakes on a car. They help us gain control over our lives and restore homeostasis to our bodies and minds. Niyamas are like the steering wheel and the accelerator, giving us direction and energy. A car without fully functional brakes, steering wheel and accelerator will not get you to your destination and will be dangerous to drive.

Similarly, if we have checks and balances in our lives it becomes easier to maintain our equilibrium and reach our destination.

Yamas and Niyamas were also described by the scientific scholar Patanjali in his famous work, the *Yoga Sutras*. His system only included ten Yamas and Niyamas, whereas in the *Srimad Bhagavatam* twenty-four are mentioned.

* **Srimad** – most respected; **Bhagavatam** – stories that inspire the highest

The world has changed and we are no longer living in isolated communities with little effect upon one another. We live in a global village where everything and everybody in every part of the world affects the whole. We are all interdependent on one another. This means that we can no longer live as separate entities – and survive.

This leads us to the recognition that at this time in our history we need to help the world and each other first, in order to find the fulfilment we seek. This is where the Controls and Directives described in the *Srimad Bhagavatam* come into play. We believe they are exactly what is needed for our present time. They are simple guidelines that have worked for people for thousands of years, and will undoubtedly continue to do so for millennia to come.

Chris Barrington

Director of Dru (UK)
Director of the International School of Dru Yoga

The
12
Controls

CONTROL

Non-violence

What is non-violence?

Violence is the grossest expression of humanity's baser instincts. It is simply a symptom of our discontent; yet by choosing to ignore the symptoms, we allow ourselves to be disturbed by the waves of unrest that arise from the ego.

Ask yourself:

> Do my actions reflect peacefulness?

> Do my thoughts reflect peacefulness?

> Do my very intentions reflect peacefulness?

Mahatma Gandhi once said,

> **'Non-violence is an attribute of the soul, and therefore should be practised by everybody in all affairs of life.'**

How to lead a non-violent life

Think about the way you lead your life. You will find that the 'reacting mind' and ego are difficult beasts to tame. So consider what things you allow to enter your body, heart and mind. When we associate with people who live by virtuous standards they feed us with high-minded thoughts. But when we associate with angry or violent people or when we welcome the never-ending barrage of media-violence, our minds develop these violent habits too. If we instead choose to cultivate the habit of good association and to watch and read things that nurture us, when the world shows us its dark side, we will not be drawn into dark thoughts and behaviours too. Gandhi, the great exponent of non-violence, also said:

'Not to hurt any living being is no doubt part of non-violence but it is its least expression. The principle of non-violence is hurt by every evil thought, by undue haste, by lying, by hatred, by wishing ill to anyone. It is also violated by our holding onto what the world needs.'

To aspire towards a peaceful mind and come to appreciate what peace really means, we must take our lives seriously. We have to make choices about the things we eat, the things we buy and what we watch. We need to cultivate good association, even supporting ethical organisations and not exploiting those poorer than ourselves in this beautiful world.

Why vegetarian?

Everything we put into our bodies affects us both mentally and physically. Our choice of foods either regenerates the cells of our bodies or causes them to degenerate. Like Gandhi, Mansukh's father always recommended a vegetarian diet as a means to maximum vitality, health and wellbeing. As practitioners of non-violence, it naturally follows that we would not want to harm the creatures living on the earth, in the air and in the oceans.

Today, more than a billion people worldwide are vegetarian and the health and ecological sciences have recently discovered that vegetarianism is man's best and natural diet. According to the American Dietetic Association, 'most of mankind, for most of human history, has lived on vegetarian or near-vegetarian diets.'

Medical studies prove that vegetarian food is easier to digest, provides a wider range of nutrients and imposes fewer burdens and impurities on the body. Finally, Mansukh's parents maintained that when the diet is pure, the heart and mind are also pure.

Practical hints

For the body

> Try to eat vegetarian food or at least reduce your intake of animal products.

> Cultivate consumer awareness.
> Is what you buy healthy? Is it ethical?

> Cut down on junk food and stimulants such as tea and coffee.

> Walk outside in nature every day.

> When you get angry, always bring your attention to your breath. Watch your breath and even count the breaths. You will find that the mind will calm down to a nice, balanced point. You should do this before you try to add positivity to the situation.

For the mind

> Make sure to practise deep relaxation regularly, and definitely include a few moments of relaxation before your meditation practice.

> When sitting still, focus on the area of the navel, as this helps to balance the emotional response of the

adrenals, the 'anger' glands and will diffuse the energy of anger.

Affirm

I am becoming more peaceful with each breath.

CONTROL

2

Truthfulness

Embracing what is real

Truthfulness is the means by which we see what is real and what is not. Mahatma Gandhi once said:

'Non-violence and truth are so intertwined that it is practically impossible to separate them. They are like two sides of the same coin, or rather two sides of the same, smooth, unstamped metal disk. Who can say which is the obverse, and which is the reverse? Nevertheless, non-violence is the means, truth is the end.'

Gandhi achieved all his results by living his life according to non-violence and truthfulness, just two of the Controls. Amazingly enough, as a result of awakening these two qualities all of the other Controls arose in him as well.

Truthfulness is about being real! It means seeing things the way they are. It is a gateway to knowing ourselves. The more truthful we are, with ourselves and others, the more we come to know ourselves.

We begin to recognise that much in our lives is impermanent, and that most people see the world the way they would like it to be as opposed to the way it is.

Being truthful requires courage, another of the Controls – but we must first test the truthfulness of our own thoughts, which requires constant vigilance. At first this vigilance is a great effort, but with practice it becomes a natural way of living. Primarily, truthfulness requires the willingness to be totally honest with yourself because, if you cannot do this, your degree of honesty with others must inevitably be diminished.

When you are truthful with yourself you cannot hide behind excuses and activity. Over the years we have met many people who fill their lives with so much activity, there is little time left for looking at themselves. Such people exhibit a distinct lack of self-awareness.

How direct should you be?

A well-known philosopher once said, 'You should be as strong as thunder on principle and as gentle as a flower with compassion.' If we are compassionate we will always put the needs of others first and find a way to empower them and help them to grow. Being truthful ultimately means living with integrity. It is about being *one* complete being and not a disparate collection of ideas, thoughts and desires.

Question every interaction you have.

Ask yourself:

> Was my message clear?
> Did I put the needs of the other person/people first?
> Was my intention to create something beautiful?
> Was I compassionate?

When you start to live your life in this way you will find that you sleep easier. You will wake up in the morning happy and contented, just as you were when you went to bed the night before.

Practical hints

For the body

We all know that our feelings and intentions display themselves in our body language, and that the body never lies.

Try these exercises:

> Choose a firm chair on which you can sit comfortably and allow your feet to relax onto the floor. Keeping the spine erect and the head upright, begin to relax your body.

Become aware of the weight of your body in the chair. Is your weight in the centre, or to the right, or to the left? Now affirm that you are relaxed and that your body weight is moving to the middle. Let yourself become balanced and relaxed.

Now ask yourself questions about different things in your life. If you have a hidden emotional bias over a particular issue, your weight will automatically move to one side or the other. If your weight does move, then explore how you are being untruthful with yourself about that particular issue and solutions for resolving it. When you get the right solution for you, your weight will automatically move back to the centre again. Imbalance of the body, relates directly to unbalanced emotions.

> Develop a posture that is alert. Sit with your spine elongated so that you allow the three lower energy centres to be open. Be honest with yourself. Listen to your body and not to the desires of your wanting mind.

For the mind

> Talk less and listen more. When you do speak choose your words carefully.

> To be clear in communication, spend time every day focussing upon the energy centre of communication in the throat. Feel the breath flowing through the throat.

> Remember that the communication centre awakens and becomes stronger when it is used to empower others. By empowering others, your own truthfulness grows.

CONTROL

3

Not stealing

Not stealing

When we desire something that does not belong to us, it indicates that we are not content with what we have, or more importantly, we are not content with *who* we think we are!

The nature of the ego is to grasp at everything around it. We call this grasping the 'wanting mind'. It arises from the ego and is always creating preferences for what it wants. More importantly, it is always grasping for possessions.

When you learn to be still and to listen to the mind, at first you become aware of the continual, habitual noise or chatter that it makes. With practice, and working with non-violence as we have already discussed, you will find that this noise begins to dissipate and dissolve away. At this point when we listen more deeply, we begin to sense the presence of a quiet yet insistent need. It is as if an inner voice is saying 'what next... just what is next?' This is the voice of the ego, which rules and dominates so much of our life.

When you find your mind telling you that you need something, whether it is something material or social,

or even something intensely personal, ask yourself
the following questions:

> Do I really need this?

> Do I want this for myself, or will it benefit anyone
  else?

> Be truthful with yourself – if you really need it, then
  allow yourself to have it.

You may think that this introspective process about
coveting other people's possessions, has little to
do with stealing, but be assured that by looking
at yourself in this way, you start to achieve an
understanding of the ego's grasping nature. This will
then enable you to do something about it.

In history, we find that many of the greatest thinkers
have been people of great simplicity. It seems that
once the mind becomes free from desire, space
becomes available for higher and greater thoughts.

Practical hints

For the body

> Experiment with not having particular foods just because you want them! Instead, train yourself to watch your desires and learn to distinguish them from your actual needs. You will then be able to moderate them.

> When you enter into the mode of giving, you leave the mode of wanting. Learn to give things away.

For the mind

> Learn to watch the wanting, grasping mind as it reaches out and tries to take everything.

> Whenever you find the mind grasping for something which is not yours, ask yourself the questions:

> Do I really need this?

> Do I want this for myself, or will it benefit anyone else?

> Also ask yourself why you are not content with what you have.

CONTROL

Non-attachment

Non-attachment

Our mentors taught us that the main cause of our suffering is our over-identification with who we think we are. We feel compelled to believe that our physical body is the mainstay of our existence. We think we are 90% body. Yet, at the same time our experience tells us that our mind controls the body and its functions. And even this fluctuating mind is only a limited part of who we are.

Our experience in the world at large, proves to us that our over-identification with the body occupies all our time and money, as well as our attention and emotions. In the inner recesses of our being, a spark of knowing reminds us that the major determining factor of our overall health, is our degree of self-worth.

While we must acknowledge our body and mind as major instruments of engagement with the world, at the same time, it is crucial to develop and assimilate new perspectives. These new perspectives will arise when we practise the art of non-attachment.

Once we have succeeded in establishing a relationship with our body and mind that is free from emotional clutter, the extreme swinging of our moods slows down. This stabilising of the mind-body-intellect, creates great strength and stamina. Successful access to these enormous inner reserves of energy allows us to experience a greater degree of freedom when we enter into life as it is now. It means we can participate in the fullness of life.

The most important prerequisite for success here is not to be attached to non-attachment. Avoid making it something so out-of-the-ordinary that it entraps you. Remind yourself that all techniques are given to help you experience freedom from the tyranny of your own expectations about how you would like the world to be, and how everyone should behave in it. The very act of practising non-attachment must necessarily involve correct discrimination.

The final benefit of learning to act from a point of non-attachment, is that we are able to live in full awareness of who we are – because it is we who give meaning and fullness to any event or experience in life.

Practical hints

For the body

> The absence of sense organs does not lessen our true human value. Notice how people who are blind, deaf or lame are still able to lead a fully functioning emotional and intellectual life.

> Think of Helen Keller and the enormous contribution she made to our understanding of how we are in the world despite her profound physical disabilities.

For the mind

> Learn to live in this moment through the practice of meditation.

> Contemplate the transient states of the human body from infancy through to maturity and old age, in times of illness and disease as well as in good health.

CONTROL

5

Humility

Removing the shadow from your life

When we experience times of happiness and unhappiness in our lives, we often use the words light and dark to describe them. We were once sitting with Chhaganbhai Patel, Mansukh's father, who was explaining about the darkness that people experience in their lives. He looked at us and said,

> 'You know, there is another way – and that is to bring yourself closer to the ground. When you are low to the ground, the shadow appears so much smaller too!'

But what does it mean to bring yourself close to the ground, to remove the shadow from your life?
It means making yourself humble.

Ask yourself these questions:

> Do you always need to have the last word?

> Are you concerned about how you appear to others?

> Do you spend time thinking how good you are at a particular thing?

Treat all things equally

Being humble means having a realistic view of your
own strengths, while recognising that each person
you meet will have their own equally good, if not better
skills. Many of the scriptures of the world talk about the
importance of treating all beings equally. Being humble
means that your ego is not colouring your view of life.
Humility does not mean that you do not see your own
self worth, but that you see the worth of others as well.

Gandhi was one of the humblest men of the last century,
with no illusions as to what he could achieve. He made
this very clear when he said,

> 'I have not the shadow of a doubt that any man
> or woman can achieve what I have, if he or she
> would make the same effort and cultivate the
> same hope and faith.'

Mansukh's parents were two of the humblest people
you could ever meet. They would give you anything
they had, yet they were the most noble of people, with
a nobility that was born of strength of both spirit and
humility. Saint Francis of Assisi was also a very humble
man, yet his strength of vision led him to establish

a spiritual order that has lasted for more than six hundred years.

What are the prerequisites for humility?

To be humble we need to have tamed the wanting mind. Our thoughts need to become peaceful. In other words, the previous Controls need to have awakened in us and become our friends. To develop humility, we must attempt to do good works and yet not need to take credit for them. When generosity becomes second nature and we do not seek recognition for it, then humility has found a place in us.

Practical hints

For the body

> Dress simply yet with dignity.

> Give gifts anonymously.

For the mind

> In meditation, focus on the heart centre, situated behind the sternum. It is related to the cardiac plexus and the thymus gland, the 'immune system controller'.

> Use the following Heart Meditation to access your heart energy:

Sit quietly and let your body relax. Deepen your breathing and slow it down slightly. Follow the breath into your chest on the in-breath, and follow it out again as you exhale. Slowly gather your awareness into the centre of the chest.

Visualise the heart as a point of light in the centre of your chest. Feel that joy emanates from this point as you breathe out, and feel the joy permeating your whole body.

CONTROL

6

Non-possessiveness

Non-possessiveness and removal of clutter

Non-possessiveness happens when we simplify and remove the clutter from our lives. It arises from non-attachment. All the possessions we have around us ultimately affect the degree of clarity that we have. In many respects a tidy and ordered environment can help create a tidy, ordered mind.

Many years ago Mansukh's father, Chhaganbhai, told us that when we have possessions, we invest part of our energy into them. Consequently, the more we possess, and the more energy we put into the things around us, the less there is available for the process of self-transformation.

An illustration

There is an old story about a wandering monk who came to the palace of a wise king. Once he was granted an audience, the monk commented that the king had such opulence around him that there was no way that he could ever develop spiritually. The monk then told the king that he would have to renounce all his possessions because it was the only way to achieve happiness – by becoming free of his attachment to them. The king, who had no attachment to his kingdom smiled and said: 'I agree with you, in fact let's do it now.'

The monk was quite taken aback at this very free response, and even more surprised when the king exchanged all of his finery for the robes of a simple monk. As they walked out of the palace together and away from the city, the monk suddenly remembered that he had left his begging bowl in the palace. He panicked, insisting that they return straight away to retrieve this, his only possession. The king looked at the monk in amazement. 'After all that I have given up today, can you not even let go of your begging bowl?'

The point of this simple story is that attachment is not related to the size or quantity of our possessions. Something small can bind us just as much as a whole kingdom. In fact, the king showed himself to be the wiser man.

Chhaganbhai, Mansukh's father, told us how this had been taught to him with the following verse from the great classic, the *Bhagavad Gita*, a beautiful poem of seven hundred verses, renowned the world over for its profound wisdom:

> 'Bound on every side by a network of desires,
> absorbed in lust and anger, they pursue money
> dishonestly for the satisfaction of their cravings.
> "Today I got this," they say, "and tomorrow I
> shall get that. This is mine and that will also
> soon be mine." '

Ask yourself these questions:

> Is my home cluttered with un-necessary things?
> How many of the clothes in my wardrobe do I really
>   need? How often do I wear them anyway?

One way of defining possessiveness is 'to take more
than you need or have a right to.' Considering this
further, greed often goes deeper than physical
possessions. At social events do you go out of your way
to make your point, or interrupt others just so you can
have more than your fair share of time or attention?

Learn to be charitable, and to give more of your
time and self. Remember the old maxim that says,
'Whatever it is that you want, you should first give.'
This means that if you want love, you should first give
love. If you want wealth and opulence, this you should
give. Finally, if you want the ultimate, then you have to
be prepared to give everything.

Practical hints

For the body

> Try this heart opening breath:

  Lie down on the ground, on your back.

  Bending your knees, bring your feet close to your hips and rest them on the ground.

  Breathe in, while you raise your arms up and over your head to rest on the ground behind you. Stretch at the top of the breath, and as you breathe out, bring the arms back down by your sides.

  Repeat several times.

For the mind

> Every day make a list of people you will give a small gift to. You will find great excitement in the process of wrapping and giving your gifts.

> A very dear friend of ours was given a whole collection of presents on her birthday. As soon as she had received them, she handed all of the gifts out again randomly, without even opening them. It was a big lesson for people in the room, seeing their presents being given away immediately.

CONTROL

7

Respect for principles that empower us

Respect for principles that empower us

No matter who we are, we each impose a structure upon our lives. Because we are creatures of habit, it is very natural for us to create rules for how we live. Usually, by trial and error, or through good teaching we find a set of rules that work for us. Children are taught to dress, wash, clean their teeth after eating, and many other things.

Often the principles upon which we base our lives do not empower us, but in fact create disharmony.

Principles that empower us fall into two categories:

> principles that regulate our lives, and
> key principles that enable our lives to flow in the direction we would like to go in.

Classic examples of key principles at work, are the martial arts and other forms of movement, that involve intense mental as well as physical discipline. Each of the martial arts has a set style or set of movements that focus the mind and build the body's agility, flexibility and strength. Only when the basics are learnt, is it possible to teach the student the deeper aspects of the art.

These are key techniques that would not be taught to students below a particular skill level.

In our lives this Control tells us to give respect to those key principles that work for us, and build success however we define it. Very often we use these principles, but do not obtain the best from them. If we cultivate respect for them, then we treat these principles in a more dignified way.

Practical hints

For the body

It is clear that these kind of principles are unique to the individual and that what works for one person will not necessarily work for someone else.

> Make a list of your strengths. With each strength write down one thing that you do, physically, that adds to that strength. It could be something as simple as always taking a deep breath before you go on stage, or doing some calming yoga movements before going to work.

> Ask yourself what you can do to turn your weaknesses into strengths?

For the mind

The power of our intention is directly related to the purposefulness with which we live our lives.
The more purpose there is, the greater the intention that guides it.

> Check to see how much purpose there is in your daily list of tasks. Now consider how each of those actions will help you achieve your goals, and what key principles you will use to empower your actions.

CONTROL

8

Living the highest

Living in awareness of the highest

What is the highest? Quite simply, it means living with oneness, unity, and having a vision, which goes beyond the mundane. Living with such an awareness means developing a living, growing relationship with something we can call the 'Field of Consciousness', the underlying intelligence or sub-stratum of life. For this to happen we have to assume that we possess a spark of that field which is, in effect, our own individual Self.

Identifying the Self

We have all experienced this Self. Think back to those special moments in your life when you felt connected to the whole – it could have been in times of great sorrow or elation, or when you felt a timeless, spacious contentment. It is that feeling that there is something truly amazing about your existence. You feel 'stirred to the depths of your being', knowing with full certainty, that everything is perfect.

These experiences often come upon us when we least expect them – when we are in the depths of despair. They may just arise out of the blue for no apparent reason. They tell us that somewhere deep inside us there is a very pure essence of something that lies beyond matter or energy and yet is inextricably linked to it all.

Discovering the highest through meditation

Meditation, assisted by correct posture, correct understanding and application of the art of breathing, is one of the most rewarding activities that a human being can engage in. It is the single most important method that leads us to discover the highest.

The benefits are so numerous that it would qualify for entry in the *Guinness Book of Records* – for the most potent and healing technique known to man! This time-honoured practice, is now part of the life of almost every successful man and woman upon this earth.

The ability to relax and let go is a marvellous gift. Young children are often seen to day-dream, becoming almost fixed in non-doing and non-being. It is as if they have left this world and gone to another. Adults are often puzzled or irritated by this and may shake the youngster to 'bring him or her back'. In fact the child has entered a wonderful healing state of pure meditation – one which stabilises and strengthens. It allows stress to be defused and all problems to become manageable. Immunity is boosted and health improved in this way.

Meditation not only enhances our physiological and psychological wellbeing, but it also enables us to connect with the 'Field', or whatever you would like to call it. One gains clarity about the fundamental questions: who am I and why am I here?

Meditation brings our whole existence into balance with the laws of nature. Everything that needs to be seen, felt and experienced comes forth and everything that is transient or a blurred reflection of the truth, is allowed to go its own way.

Meditation brings about a heightened awareness of life. At the same time, it enables its 'hearer' to move across different experiences and states of consciousness with ease and joy. A true shift in perception takes place. Then comes the discovery of the highest. It is impossible to say how long it takes to move from meditating on the highest as separate from 'me', to finally arriving at a living experience of the highest and 'me' as being one and the same. In this state of realisation, there is no dividing wall between the two. There is no space where we are not and the highest is – or vice versa.

This conclusion, the end of all duality, does not mean that the world vanishes or that we 'go up in a puff of smoke'. The world is still here and so are we. But now everything is connected, an undivided, seamless whole which has no edges or corners. This is a natural state to be in. We feel that all life, including our own, is full of miracles and possibilities.

Rays of awareness

It is said that our awareness shines out like rays from the five senses of the body, and that our natural habit is to measure our existence by the reflections that we get back from the objects that these rays touch. So we take happiness to be the reflection of pleasure, and unhappiness to be the reflection of pain, in some form. When we perceive the rays of awareness shining out in this way, it becomes very difficult to focus them back to the source of consciousness – to that point where we can witness or experience the highest.

Focus on the source, not the object

It is a great help in the process, if from moment to moment, you make a choice to watch the rays of awareness as they come from the source. This is instead of letting the awareness be distracted by the reflections, as they come back from the objects.

As an example, if you go to the cinema, do you find that you get drawn into the story and do not notice the passage of time during the film? You even begin to lose the awareness that you are watching a film at all. Instead, your whole attention is focused on the screen in front of you.

To begin to move towards the highest, in the cinema, you need to keep your awareness on you, watching the film, all the way through the performance. If you can do this, you will find that your discrimination improves, and you never lose sight of your true self.

When you try this in the cinema, you will see how captivating the story is, and you will find yourself being drawn into it again and again. The more you bring your awareness back to your true self the easier it becomes. You begin to be less enticed by the seductive tastes of the reflections, and more drawn to the pure joy of the source, the Field.

Take it easy

Our advice is to please take it easy. Just begin by watching where your awareness goes. When you begin to experience a little of the joy of the Field, you may discover that it is contagious. Then you will begin to make conscious choices to move towards the highest. When you begin to want the experience of the highest you will find that it is not so far away.

Practical hints

For the body

> Walk out in nature by yourself.

> While you enjoy the walk, keep your awareness on the 'you' that is enjoying the walk.

For the mind

> Try this meditation:

Sit or lie still and focus on the sense of touch. Let your awareness expand into the whole of your body, encompassing all of your skin. This will take some practice. When you have mastered this, let your awareness slowly reach out into the space around your body.

Take your time: if you practise regularly it will probably take several weeks for this to work. When it does you will feel a connectedness with your surroundings that you have never felt before.

To come out, focus on feeling the ground under you and slowly stretch to reawaken your sense of your physical body.

CONTROL

9

Silence

Silence

To reap the benefits of silence it is necessary to practise silence. Practising silence means learning to listen more than we speak. And that means we need to listen even to our own words. If we do not taste our words before they leave us, how can we be sure of the flavour that is being given to the people we are speaking to?

Sit still and listen to the sounds around you. Begin, if you like, by listening to the traffic or the sounds of the garden, or people moving in the distance. Now listen to the sounds closer to you, until finally you can even hear the sound of your own heart beating or your breath as it enters and leaves your nostrils.

When you first sit still, your sensitivity to silence increases. Noises that normally wouldn't bother you become almost intolerable as your degree of stillness increases. Finally you enter a space where there is such a beautiful silence and stillness, that you begin to hear what the ancients referred to as 'the unstruck sound' – the sound that arises out of the Field of awareness itself.

We were taught by our mentors that with the right concentration and awareness, by listening to the sound of someone's voice, everything becomes known about that person; we can hear the song of their soul. But even if we do not have that degree of concentration, we can still listen so intently that we discover something beautiful about them.

In the ancient science of sound, one of the beautiful facts that has come down to us is that the energy centre of hearing, the real focus point for sound, is also the centre that we can use to help to remove addictions from our lives. The link between the removal of addictions and the centre of hearing is a subtle one, that is partly explained by the change in consciousness that comes when we shift the focus from our sense of sight to one of the other senses.

Most information is processed through our eyes, and so the sense of sight dominates our lives. Very few people can listen just with the sense of hearing. You may try, but you will probably listen to the sounds and use them to build up a mental picture of the space around you. In other words, you are so used to the dominance of your sense of sight, that it even dominates your mental perception. Even the word imagination comes from the word 'image'.

With practice, however, it is possible to shift the dominance from one sense to another, first with the use of the imagination and by using the sense in a pure way. When we can do this, we begin to free ourselves from those things that we are addicted to. This is the starting point for the immense depth that exists in the world of sound, but this world is only available to us when we are able to shift the focus of sense domination from that of sight to that of hearing. This can only be done when we are prepared to explore silence.

Practical hints

For the body

> Try this practice to develop your sense of hearing:

Take a sheet of paper and a pencil and sit outside in nature. At the centre of the piece of paper put a circle to represent *you*. Then close your eyes and listen. Every time you hear a sound, locate it with your hearing, and put a symbol on the paper to represent the sound. Slowly you will fill up the sheet of paper with symbols representing the different sounds around you. You will find that in even half an hour, your hearing will become very acute.

For the mind

> Choose at least one day every month when you can be completely silent, either for all or part of the day. At first, this may seem almost impossible within your busy schedule, but you will need to be firm with yourself, even if it means going for a walk in order to get your silent space. While you are silent, carry a notebook and pen with you so that you can record ideas as they come to you.

You will come to really value this special, silent time.

CONTROL

10

Steadiness

Steadiness

Being steady means being firm in your intentions
and unaffected by the things that life throws at you.
Steadiness is not about rigidity. Like a tree that stands
strong in the wind, steadiness is about bending and
moving while remaining rooted firmly to the earth.
A tree that becomes too rigid, will break when the
wind blows.

Steadiness means you are a rock for others to lean
on, where they can take shelter from the storms of
life. Your unwavering balance attracts others to you
because they know that they can trust your stability. In
many ways this kind of steadiness happens when you
have practised drawing the rays of your mind back in
towards the source of your awareness. So we see that
the prerequisite for steadiness, is the cultivation of a
quiet, non-reactive mind.

Ask yourself these questions:

> How am I affected by people's words?

> How reactive am I?

> How much am I ruled by what the world presents to
  me, rather than by who I am?

It is important to think about these issues. Earlier we spoke about living with an awareness of the highest and this is a fundamental requirement for attaining steadiness.

To be steady requires inner strength that flows from a sense of conviction about what you are doing. To remain steady requires strength, just as strength is required to hold the physical body still. The stronger you are, the easier it is to hold a posture and when you have inner strength, steadiness comes naturally. Cultivate steadiness and you will begin to see the world as it is and not how you would like it to be.

Practical hints

For the body

> To develop steadiness in the body stand in the
Mountain posture as follows:

Stand still with your feet hip width apart. Slowly
lengthen your spine. Straighten your legs without
locking them. Tuck your tailbone under to lengthen
the lower spine and pull the abdomen back to hold
the posture firm.

Lift the sternum and relax your shoulders and
arms. Looking neither up nor down, pull your
chin back very slightly to lengthen the neck. Feel
as though there is a string attached to the crown
of your head pulling you up. Enjoy the stillness
and stability of this posture for as long as you feel
comfortable.

For the mind

> Try this breathing practice:

Standing in the Mountain pose, breathe in and let your awareness rise up through your body from the ground to the heart. As you breathe out, let it rise up, through the crown of your head to the heavens.

As you breathe in again, let your awareness be drawn in through the crown of the head, back to the heart. As you breathe out, feel it descend back down into the earth. Repeat this process until you feel a strong sense of stillness.

Stand in this stillness keeping your awareness flowing with the breath.

CONTROL

Patience

Patience – forbearance

Gandhi began his campaign to free India from British rule in the first few years of the last century, yet it took over thirty years of continuous effort to achieve the independence of India in 1947. From steadiness comes patience. He was willing to wait for decades for the right time or situation to present itself.

Being patient is not just about waiting. It arises from an inner stillness and certainty regarding the result that you wish to see. If you wish to develop patience you should ask yourself how well you have developed the other Controls.

Ask yourself the following questions:

> Do you get frustrated when you have to wait?
> Do you get irritated by other people and the way that they do things?

Technology makes us slaves to time

Modern western society places much emphasis upon technology that slices time into smaller and smaller portions. Computers on desks in most households in the western world, have internal clocks running at over a thousand million pulses per second. The amount of information that is available at the touch of a button or the click of a mouse, is phenomenal. With the increase in the availability of instant information, we become used to the speed and are intolerant when we don't get fast results. We become slaves to time. At school, our children live by the timetable. When we work in the world we clock-in and clock-out. In the end we become so caught in the flow of having to work to deadlines, that the very time that we use to regulate our lives, becomes a cage from which we cannot escape.

Young children are naturally free from dependence on time. They live in the moment. Even tomorrow is too far away for them. Do you remember how long the summers were when you were a child? There is a freshness in the child's view that is not concerned for the future, only the present. As we get older we lose this, and time seems to rush away from us. Everyone is so concerned to do things as quickly as they can. People become impatient with taxi-drivers if they can't get to their destination in five minutes instead of seven.

Taking patience to a deeper level

Another word to describe this Control is, forbearance. This word goes deeper than simple patience. It is patience with strength, with steadiness, with self-control, with mercy, and with leniency. In fact, forbearance in many ways, sums up the whole of the Controls so far. Practise forbearance and it is said that all things become possible.

There are many stories in every tradition of how we do not succeed until we let go of our expectations in the moment, and embrace the present with joy.

Practical hints

For the body

> Practise this Acceptance Meditation:

When you sit still, practising the art of the quiet mind, notice the games that the body and the mind play with you. At first the ego will use the weapon of impatience against you. Learn to be still and watch the thoughts as they cross the sky of your mind. The symptoms of this impatience can be sensations in the body, an intense need to move, or a sense of discomfort. If this happens, gently stretch yourself without losing the quietness, and then sink back into the stillness once more. As you practise each day, you will find that your body will get used to the stillness. Once the reactions from the body cease, you will find that you are able to sit still quite peacefully for longer periods of time.

The beauty of this practice is that it enables you to see how the mind reacts to different situations. A sensitivity to the mind's reactivity is a very useful quality to develop. Our problem is that in everyday life we react to things all the time and we do not even know it.

For the mind

To move forward in life we have to cultivate patience that arises out of an acceptance of where we are in our life. We also need to cultivate the vision to know where we are going in the future.

> Practise the Acceptance Meditation to help you have patience with yourself. If you do not have patience with yourself, how can you expect to have patience with others, or other situations in your life?

CONTROL

12

Courage

Courage

Last of the Controls but by no means least, courage is the key to so many things in life. Gandhi said,

> 'Non-violence and cowardice go ill together. I can imagine a fully armed man to be at heart a coward. Possession of arms implies an element of fear, if not cowardice. But true non-violence is an impossibility without the possession of unadulterated fearlessness.'

If we couple the disciplines we have spoken about so far with courage, they are guaranteed to succeed. It is only possible to be completely fearless, however, when you have recognised that you are part of something much bigger – part of a universal consciousness. Carl Jung called it the *Collective Unconsciousness*.

There is only love and fear

It has been said by many teachers, both ancient and modern, that there are only two emotions in life – fear and love. All other emotions are manifestations of these two, so that anxiety is fear based in a social setting. Attachment to possessions, and particularly the drive to protect your investments, all arise out of insecurity.

Teach children to be who they are

Children are taught at school to behave 'or else' face the consequences. If children were to grow up strong and gently supported, they would be truly fearless when they got older. A system that relies on punishment and not empowerment, will not teach children to succeed. How many people just never grow up emotionally and are instead caught in the fearful state of childhood disempowerment? In fact any success that a teacher of children has ever had, is always related to making children feel good about themselves.

In order to grow at many different levels, therefore, we have to learn to connect with the Field of Consciousness.

Practical hints

For the body

> Practise the Gesture of Courage:

Stand or sit comfortably. Raise the hands until they are about three inches (10cm) in front of the shoulders, with palms facing forwards and the fingers pointing upwards. Have the elbows close in to the sides. Draw the abdomen in gently and hold it firm for a moment.

Focus upon something that creates fear in your life.

Affirm

I am strong, full of courage, and no longer afraid.

For the mind

> Make a list of the things you would like to do but are afraid to. Look closely at the reasons why you are afraid and ask:

What could happen if I actually did this?

To succeed in any endeavour entails a degree of risk. Evaluating risk is a necessary part of the adventure. But when you have decided to proceed put your whole energy to the task.

The

12

Directives

DIRECTIVE

1

External purity

External purity

Mansukh's parents taught us that it is very important
to promote health, presentation and tidiness – not just
in clothing, but also in everything we do. It is about
having an attitude of clean living. When you consider
some of the things people put into their bodies, it is
no wonder they have problems with their health.
We can only mistreat the body for so long before it
starts to complain. So it makes sense to practise
bodily cleanliness.

In the East, keeping the body clean is a public part
of life, especially in the villages. People bathe openly
in the rivers without any sense of embarrassment,
vigorously rubbing their bodies with towels to
stimulate the skin.

Eastern philosophy recommends internal cleaning
exercises to clear the sinuses and oesophagus
of mucus and there is also a complete intestinal
cleansing process.

Practising specific movements promotes strength,
flexibility and energy as well as preventing the body
from ageing.

As part of the washing process you are taught to scrape your tongue in the morning with a special tongue scraper. Keeping the tongue clean has the effect of removing bad breath, cleaning the intestinal tract and stimulating digestion.

This means taking the time to consider how you present yourself. Gandhi said, 'You may only have a simple **dhoti**, but you can wear it with dignity.'

Practical hints

For the body

> Wash completely at least once a day.

> Learn how to clean the tongue.

> Exercise at least once a day. This could be walking, swimming or some other form of exercise. Gentle movements help to strengthen the body.

> Fast on water and fruits at least one day a month. It will give your intestines a rest and time to catch up.

For the mind

> Generate an attitude of tidiness in all things. Keep your clothes tidy. Keep your environment neat, let it reflect the tidiness of your mind.

> It is said that by keeping the physical body clean we develop an understanding of the impermanent nature of the body. This in turn induces us to direct our attention towards the Self.

2

Internal purity

Purity of thoughts determines our reality

Is it not true that a healthy and pure body makes us feel better about ourselves and our future aspirations? Is it not true that purity of mind is the key to success in all our relationships? Does not the practice of sitting still and meditating, either in nature or in a quiet place at home, result in the co-creation of pure and powerful thoughts which ultimately empower every aspect of our life?

Question the world that you live in

In this world of ours we tend to ignore the need for what we call, 'sensible' purity. Just step back and take a look at the pollution in our environment; the darkening smoke on the horizon, the plastic and rubbish washed up on the shores of our oceans. Notice the never-ending mad rush in the high streets and huge 500 ton steel crates flying over the major cities of the world almost every minute.

As you observe the daily newspapers, magazines and television programmes, what do you see? How do you feel? Does it give you a sense of security? What are we giving away? What are we being given?

What do you see in the faces of young people who are desperately seeking to find true meaning to their existence? Where are they looking and who do they ask? Will they find it? Have you found it?

Where does purity of body and mind fit into all this?

The power of intention

There is a valuable lesson here for us, too. If we keep a constant check on the purity of our intention before the day begins, and then at regular intervals throughout the day, we will have an accurate guide to whether we are still on course or not. When something goes wrong, stop and review what has happened. You will almost certainly discover that impurity has somehow crept into your thoughts. But within minutes, you can adjust your course and sail on towards a completely successful and joyful day. It's worth a try!

Practical hints

For the body

> Keeping the body clean, both internally and externally, promotes good health and clarity of mind.

> Every so often we find ourselves in an extremely negative environment, or one where there are a lot of emotional people. When we come away from it, we find somehow the emotionality tends to stick to us. One way of cleansing yourself is to have a salt shower.

> Take a container of salt into the shower with you, and rub it into your body as you wash. Afterwards, shower normally to take the salt off the body. You will find that your energy will be completely different and you will not be so tired.

For the mind

> Take part in activities that promote social justice.

> Try to avoid spending too much time in the
  presence of those who are angry or continually
  upset. If you do come into the presence of anger
  or emotionality, always spend a few moments
  afterwards walking on the earth. You will feel
  renewed by it.

> Every so often, sleep outside on the earth. You will
  find that nothing refreshes you as much as this.

DIRECTIVE

3

Singing power words

Singing power words

A power word is a phrase or word that is sung repeatedly in order to bring a particular state of consciousness to the singer. This Directive is one of the most ancient and well known means of achieving a state of meditation.

But when we talk about singing a power word as a Directive we are referring to the vibrations that attune the mind to the infinite space of consciousness. Of course, we can use a word like peace or joy. The vibrations of these words however, can only bring to you the symptoms of these qualities, not their essence.

In the singing of power words, ancient languages are more potent than most modern languages. Consider Sanskrit, which has fifty letters or basic sounds. In Eastern philosophy, these sounds are spread throughout the body, shown autistically as being written on the petals of lotuses. Modern European languages with a narrower range of sounds, only activate certain parts of the body. Therefore, the full range of sound possibilities is almost never realised.

Other, more general power words, are taught to awaken certain qualities in our life.

Just think for a moment. Contemplate upon the creative or destructive power of words. Your choice of words can bring about either sadness, unhappiness, joy, or laughter. Imagine what you could achieve if your words were infused with the energy and intention of the very highest.

Practical hints

For the body

The following sounds have been useful for centuries to improve the health of the different internal organs in the body.

heart	**oo**	neck/joints	**ooaa**
liver	**cha**	eyes	**haa**
gall bladder	**mmmm**	thyroid	**ohh**
kidneys	**shh**	spleen	**thaa**
lungs	**waa**	bladder	**raa**
knees/hips	**vaa**	pancreas	**fa**
central nervous system	**ee**		

You may intone them silently, in a whisper, or out loud.

For the mind

The most ancient and well known power word is the great word **Om**, or Amen.

> Sing this quite loudly to start with then slowly become quieter and quieter until you are singing internally. Gradually allow even the internal sound to fade into stillness while breathing normally.

> Take a deep breath and repeat.

DIRECTIVE

Creative discipline

Creative discipline

Applying creative discipline is like tempering steel. It is a process of inner strengthening.

If we wish to succeed at anything in life we will have to work for it. As the saying goes, 'There's no such thing as a free lunch.' If we want to do well at sports, we have to train. If we want to do well in our examinations we have to study hard. Every situation in life that we want to succeed in requires hard work. This 'hard work for personal success' is what we call creative discipline.

Ask yourself why personal development should be any different from any other area of your life. The clue is, that when we work hard in *any* area of our life, it somehow moulds our character. We grow as people through developing some part of ourselves. Imagine then how the process is speeded up when we apply the hard work, the creative discipline, to developing *specific* areas in our lives.

However, we can take the process too far. Take for example the story of Prince Siddhartha, who later became the Buddha. After renouncing his princely life, he lived in the forest with a group of renunciates and practised severe disciplines over a long period of time.

One day, he was sitting under a tree by a river when he heard the voices of some people passing by in a boat. One voice belonged to a man teaching a student to tune a stringed instrument. He heard the teacher say, 'If you tighten the string too much it will break, but if you do not tighten it enough, you cannot play it.' Hearing these words, Siddhartha suddenly realised that his disciplines were too harsh and were not leading him anywhere. He immediately stopped and vowed to find a path to realisation that followed a middle way.

In the Far East the practice of creative discipline develops spiritual strength and we often hear of saints who underwent creative discipline to bring a benefit to themselves or to the world.

Mansukh's father would always ask us to fast on very simple foods when we stayed with them for the weekend. He told us that this would guarantee the success of our studies.

He explained that there is a different quality to the power of creative discipline when we apply it to the process of reaching the highest in life. *This* kind of hard work brings the universe onto your side.

Practical hints

For the body

> Practise fasting. Either eat simple foods, or perhaps fast by eating only once that day.

For the mind

Keeping it to yourself, make an agreement with the universe that you will:

> Do good to one person each day without their knowledge.

> Sing a definite number of power words each day.

> Make a commitment to keep to a fixed time each day for your meditation practice.

DIRECTIVE

5

Making life sacred

Making life sacred

When we live our life with sacredness, by implication we make it special. Normally sacredness is associated with the word 'holy,' but Mansukh's parents taught us to relate it to celebration. If every moment can be seen as celebratory, then somehow many of the things that drag us into lower, more negative states, no longer seem to affect us in the same way.

To see the truth of this statement we just have to look into our own experiences and compare the good days with the bad. When things go well for us a kind of elation fills us. Whatever comes our way we seem to be able to deal with it.

On the bad days however, everything is a problem. The most trivial issues become blown up out of proportion and by the end of the day we can sometimes feel that perhaps it would have been better for everyone if we had simply stayed in bed!

The problem and the solution lie with *us*.

In the end, it all boils down to how we approach the day. Do we enter into it with celebration and joy, or do we fight it, tooth and nail, for the slim pickings that it will give us?

When we can view life as something worthy of celebration, it allows us to find joy where we normally find problems. But the most beautiful aspect of this Directive is, that we are not to keep our joy to ourselves. Instead, we must let as many people as we can share in the delight of the celebration. When we make a party of it, we soon see that everyone else's energy and enthusiasm is lifted as well.

Think of celebration as applying your creative discipline to bring everyone else into the same attitude of joy. If we are all moving in the same direction then life becomes very easy. Of course, to achieve this often requires very skilful use of our creative discipline, and sometimes we may feel as though we are herding cats!

Above all, our own attitude of celebration should be unassailable. After all, no moment in our life is ever repeated, and each one is precious.

Practical hints

For the body

> Do things spontaneously for others. Help others by giving the gifts of your time, thoughts, and energy.

> Do what is practical, but try not to miss an opportunity to bring someone into the specialness of your celebration of life.

For the mind

> Make sure you take time every day to think of who you would like to include in your celebration of life, and how you will actually make it happen.

DIRECTIVE

6

Making life sacred

Faith

Faith is the pillar on which all of the other Directives stand firm. It is a complete and utter trust in the universe, or the power of life itself. It means that there is purpose behind every event in your life and that everything is exactly as it should be.

Why then is faith such a difficult thing to achieve? Most people, if asked, would probably admit that their faith is more like a chink in the armour of their doubt.

Working in partnership with the universe

Faith is not about passing the responsibility for your life over to the universe. It is actually about taking full responsibility for your life, in the knowledge that together, you make an amazing team. Even on a human scale, when you cultivate faith within a companionship or friendship, somehow it draws the very highest out of you both.

So how do we do it? Begin by learning to have a dialogue with nature. It is in nature that life shows us its beauty. Try to get outside and admire the beauty around you. Begin to recognise the miracle of nature, and you will begin to feel a different kind of attunement in your life. Bring this dialogue into your everyday life. Whenever you have a spare moment, take the time to renew this relationship.

Most people think of faith as a quality that arises in us because we have been a witness to the miraculous, a gift given by some grace. In actual fact, faith has to be practised in order for it to work for us. Like all things in life, for something to grow strong in us, we need to make an effort to build it. Faith is the same. It is important to remember that we should not try to lift something beyond our strength. Building up to it, eventually faith becomes a way of life.

Having faith means that we have trust, but to test our trust, we have to be able to listen to the still inner voice and follow its instruction.

A man shouts up to Heaven,'Show yourself to me and I'll do anything for you.' A voice comes down from the heavens 'I am here!' The man looks sheepishly up and says 'Just testing...' The voice replies, 'Likewise!'

Faith is a two-way process. There has to be a dialogue between us and the universal intelligence. We have to be prepared to listen too!

Practical hints

For the body

> Adopt the following posture of faith:

Sit or stand erect without leaning forward. Raise
the sternum and pull in the upper abdomen slightly.
Without looking up, pull the chin back very lightly.
Bring the hands together as if praying, but keep
a space between them. Now focus on that space
between the hands.

For the mind

Remember, that in order to be practical, set aside time
every day to think about and consider your exploration
into these Controls and Directives. In the context of
faith, ask yourself the following questions:

> Have I had an internal dialogue with the universe
today?

> What is my vision for the next year? What will I do
today that will bring me closer to my vision for the
next year?

In your internal dialogue with the universe, ask for its
advice. Listen to the still quiet voice, and act upon the
answer you receive.

DIRECTIVE

7

Hospitality

Hospitality

The hospitality of people in the third world is legendary. When visitors come to your home in the villages in India, they are treated as revered guests. This was the first lesson that we ever learned from Mansukh's parents.

As complete strangers, we were welcomed into their house and treated with such respect. Actually, when we watched Mansukh's parents, I noticed that they took this concept even further. Instead of waiting for someone to arrive at the doorstep, everyone they met was treated as someone very special.

This means applying complete hospitality to whoever comes in front of us.

Mansukh's father told us that no one should ever leave you empty-handed, for there is always something to give them in this moment. This goes beyond charity.

When we practise seeing the highest in all beings, we recognise a connection, a commonality that exists between us and the rest of the world. We realise that when we hurt someone else, in the end we are only hurting ourselves. And when we see the highest in all beings, whoever they are, and whatever they do to us, we see the highest within ourselves.

Stories abound throughout history of saints who lived their lives seeing nothing but the highest in the people in front of them. From Saint Francis of Assisi, who was a friend to all creatures, to Saint Jalaram in Gujarat who was renowned for feeding thousands and thousands of people during his lifetime. How much they were loved.

When we can see the highest in everyone we meet, then we find that we actively work to bring it out of others. We become grateful to meet people, because of the joy we can find in bringing out the very best in them.

Being hospitable arises from this same attitude – that the most important person in your life is about to arrive. Are you ready for them? What gifts will you give to them? How can you help them?

When we begin to think in this way, the gift of true hospitality becomes ours. In fact, it is such an amazing gift, because the more we give it away, the stronger it becomes in us.

Practical hints

For the body

> To be hospitable, always keep your home as you would like it if the most special person in your life was about to arrive.

> Give food to the poor or homeless on a regular basis.

For the mind

> Whoever you meet, whether they be friend, stranger or adversary, greet them with the mental thought, 'What if this is someone dear to me in disguise?' Then act as if it were the case.

DIRECTIVE

8

Silent gratitude

Silent gratitude

Mother Teresa was once delivering a talk in front of thousands of people. As she came down from the podium after giving her presentation, a woman thrust out her hand and pulled at her garment. 'Mother,' she said pitiably, 'My baby is dying. What can I do?' Mother Teresa looked at the woman with infinite compassion and said,

> **'God has given you the gift of a beautiful little baby. If he wants you to give it back to him, please do so with grace and gratitude.'**

Gratitude is something we are not really familiar with in our society, unless for some reason, someone very close to us is spared from a disaster of some kind. It is, however, quite possible to feel that same sense of gratitude all the time. This is the feeling that enables us to celebrate life.

Why is it that it often takes tragedy and suffering to make us put our hands together in prayer? Is it simply that we are such creatures of habit, that we easily get used to the comfort of feeling happy and forget to be grateful?

Try it now:

Just stop for a moment and express your gratitude to the universe for all the beauty around you and the gifts you have been given this day – whether they are comfortable or uncomfortable.

It is important to ask for the right things in life. If all of your attention goes on making money and providing for your family (who are worthy of gratitude in many ways) then that is the limit to which your life will rise. The more you can create a dialogue with the universe, the more you will find that you will gain opportunities to rise to your true heritage.

Practical hints

For the body

> Stand or sit while holding the gesture of praying
  hands. Focus on the attitude of first creating a
  dialogue with the highest as we have discussed.
  Allow that dialogue to be filled with gratitude
  for creation.

For the mind

> It is wonderful to express gratitude for being alive.

> Once we can accept everything as it is, and that all
  is perfect, there can only be a sense of gratitude for
  the perfection in each moment.

DIRECTIVE

9

Power of walking

The power of walking

Walking is a magnificent synthesis of physical health, mental clarity, emotional freedom and spiritual awakening. It provides the perfect tool for creating a happy, balanced human being. It is said that when you walk, your strength and fortune walk with you. One of the greatest gifts it provides is that of simplicity. When you walk you cannot carry your settee or television or any possessions! You only have yourself and your connection to nature and the wider universe.

There are many benefits to walking. Firstly it is a means of generating health and vitality within the body through the movement of activity. The stimulation of the nerve endings on the feet activates energy flow throughout the body. Leg muscles are toned, the spine is gently rocked, and energy spirals up through the spine. Deeper breathing is encouraged, which cleanses the blood and calms and clears the mind.

Walking in nature allows us to absorb negative ions, which also act as a stimulator of fresh energy and aliveness. The highest level of negative ions exists by the ocean, open plains and valleys and near waterfalls and trees. There are very few in urban situations. Walking is therefore far better in a rural setting. It is a means of taking time out to gain perspective on your life and also acts as a means of encouraging the body to regain its natural circadian rhythm. It gives us the opportunity to be exposed to natural light which activates the pineal gland, the body's light meter. This in turn stimulates the major systems in the body, creating a tremendous feeling of wellbeing. The companionship of walking is also a great way to get to know someone.

It is even more special when we walk to a place of special significance to us or to society in general. If we give our walk meaning, then its transforming power is enhanced by the energy of the places we visit. The major religions of the world all have pilgrimage routes, based around visiting sacred places. There are awe-inspiring places in the world that have their own special energy, too. Places like the Grand Canyon, Niagara Falls, and Uluru (Ayers Rock) in Australia are all visited by millions of people.

Practical hints

For the body

> The main key to walking is to lift the body upwards
  and forwards. The hips face squarely forward and
  should be fairly level with one another. Feet face
  forward because facing outwards they can create
  lower back, knee, ankle and foot problems.

> It is important to try to have good core support –
  with your pelvic floor and transversus abdominis
  muscles gently engaged – as you stride forward.
  This prevents sideways movement of the hips which
  could put the whole spine out of alignment and
  affect energy flow. Let your arms swing naturally by
  your sides.

For the mind

Whilst on our Eurowalk 2000 peace walking tours we
discovered how visualisation can help you to walk
upright with a greater sense of purpose.

> Visualise a golden cord extending from your navel
  towards a point on the horizon and then look ahead
  to that point as you walk towards it.

> When you dedicate the purpose of your walking
> to some ideal such as world peace or with the
> intention of helping someone in need, it gives
> tremendous strength to your step as well as having
> a transforming effect on you as a person. It is
> based on the principle that you, as an individual, do
> make a difference.

People have walked for peace since time immemorial.
The Nipponzan Myohoji monks, the Peace Pilgrim,
Gandhi and even Jesus and his disciples, are
examples of this attitude of purposeful walking.
If we wish to tune into the power of walking, it is
important to give our walk a meaning, otherwise it
becomes just recreation.

**'Let my feet walk firmly on the earth, my head
crowned with stars.'** Mahatma Gandhi

DIRECTIVE

10

Acting & desiring the highest

Acting and desiring the highest

After all the previous Controls and Directives one might imagine that the message would have come across by now. But there is a subtlety here that can be missed. This principle is asking us to be pro-active in seeking to serve others. This means we do not just wait for someone to come to us, but instead we think and plan how we can serve others.

An example of service

A beautiful example of service is Swami Sivananda Saraswati. He is one of India's most famous saints who died only as recently as 1960. Sivananda used to wake up at 4.00 am and plunge into the icy waters of the Ganges where he would stand in meditation for two hours until sunrise. He would then sing various purification chants before coming out of the river to meditate for a further two hours. Finally he would emerge from his simple hut, and then spend the rest of the day serving people in the most efficient and practical way he could.

Sivananda believed in the unity of all religions, and in his lifetime he wrote many scores of books, giving away hundreds of thousands of copies as gifts. One of his students who corresponded regularly received more than one thousand letters from Sivananda.

Sivananda was at his happiest when seeking out opportunities to serve others. It is such a noble way to live. We may all learn from his great example, and seek the opportunity to serve people in whatever way we can. Such service ennobles us.

It is important to remember that the more love we give away, the more we feel the presence of love in our lives. The more we give support, the more we will feel supported ourselves.

People like Swami Sivananda are rare in this world, which is why he is now regarded as one of India's greatest modern saints. However you also have the opportunity to do service to the world. Remember, it is always a matter of planning and intention. If it is your intention to serve the world, then the chances are that you will succeed.

Intention is very closely related to the power of will. If our intention is pure then we will find that all obstacles to success are removed. Our problem is that intention and expectation are two sides of the same coin. When we get caught up in the expectation that a particular thing will happen, it can dilute the power of our intention. In the end we need to be able to recognise what our expectations are – and change them into intentions.

Practical hints

For the body

> Recognise that the attitude of reaching the highest depends upon our desiring the greatest degree of health for the body too.

> Make a daily commitment to improve your health. This could include: exercise, swimming, walking, eating health promoting foods.

For the mind

> Here we need to generate an intention that we are going to always act for the good of all beings. Our expectation may be that we can only do it for part of the day, or with certain people. To make this Directive work, create an intention which says something like,

'I want to work for the good of all beings. Today this means that I will do... '

Once you have learned how to transform expectations into intentions, you will find that you have a very powerful tool for self growth.

> Reflect at the end of every day how effective the practise of this Directive was. What did you do? Did you miss any opportunity or did you take it? Evaluate what you have to work on tomorrow.

DIRECTIVE

11

Contentment

Contentment

Contentment has been described as a state of inner balance regardless of circumstances.

There is an assumption, that by practising something we will achieve happiness or contentment. It comes as quite a surprise therefore, to find contentment listed as a Directive and something that has to be practised.

Of course we know that our state of wellbeing is determined by many different factors. The food we eat, the company we keep, the things that we do and our state of health, to name but a few. It is clear that if contentment is a practice, then it is also a choice we can make from day to day, from moment to moment. This means that whatever the circumstances we find ourselves in there is always a choice as to how we can look at life.

When we make the choice to be happy and work towards contentment, we find that no matter what life puts in our way, we will always be able to find happiness.

There is an old story of a man who prayed so much that an angel appeared in front of him and offered to grant him a wish. The man considered deeply. 'What should I ask for?' he thought. 'Should I ask for wealth, health, good fortune, or long life?' He stood silently for a long time considering the question. The angel watched this and after a while gently interrupted the man's thoughts. 'May I make a suggestion?' the angel asked. The man nodded his assent and the angel said,

'Why don't you ask for a contented heart,
whatever happens to you?'

To be given contentment as a gift would be the greatest gift of all. Most of us, unfortunately, have to make a conscious choice to develop this wonderful Directive.

In order to find contentment, the most important prerequisite is to reduce the complexity of our life. When life is too complex our energy is pulled in too many different directions. There comes a point where our overall effectiveness is reduced and we start to become hyperstressed.

Remember that contentment is a choice we make from moment to moment.

Lack of contentment often arises because we feel that we have not achieved what we would have liked.

There are people who have achieved much in their lives, who are successful by everyday standards but are never content. It becomes clear that being content has nothing to do with what we possess or what we manage to achieve in our lives.

Unfortunately, when we feel that we have failed we 'beat ourselves up' and make ourselves feel worse.

Practical hints

For the body

> One way to change the emphasis from the negative
  to the positive is to remove the following words
  from our speech:

shouldn't	worry	impossible
wouldn't	doubt	hopeless
couldn't	fear	
can't	if only	
never	but	

Instead, replace them with words such as:

YES!	hope
When can I?	courage
now	easy
always	faith

For the mind

> To bring contentment into your life remind yourself
  often about the opportunities that you have, using
  the age-old practice of 'counting your blessings'.

DIRECTIVE

12

Respect for that which teaches us

Respect for that which teaches us

In the ancient text, the *Srimad Bhagavatam*, which we described at the beginning of this book, a wise teacher known as Dattatreya, is introduced as someone who had gained the respect of all who knew him. When asked who had taught him what he knew, his answer was that he had drawn all his lessons from the natural world. He said that his teachers were the elements of earth, air, fire, water and space, the sun and moon as well as many different animals and insects.

Dattatreya's descriptions contain such a deep reverence for all these things, that one cannot help but think it was that very reverence that made his connection to nature possible.

It has been our experience over the years, that everyone has something important to say, but it is only when they are treated with enough respect, that they are able to speak their most important truth.

Mansukh's parents always treated everyone they met with the greatest respect, no matter who they were. As a result people were able to open themselves up in a way they might not have been able to do with most people. When we are able to bring out the highest from people in this way, imagine what we could draw out of a person who has achieved a deeper level of consciousness.

It is one thing to talk to someone who has the keys to life. If we do not know how to approach them however, there is little chance that those keys will come our way. When we practise respecting the teacher in everyone, it guarantees that the teacher in them will become present and available to us. This, of course, takes skill and continual practice.

It is easier to find a teacher from the natural world or animal kingdom, because our egos make it very difficult to accept the truth from another person.

Practical hints

For the body

> Always carry small gifts with you, things that you can give to people you meet during the day.

> Cultivate the attitude that everyone has an important lesson for you to learn. Try to take an interest in the lives of everyone you meet and enquire of them how you can help them.

For the mind

> Every day make a list of the things you have learned from your interactions throughout the day.

> Practise the other Controls and Directives carefully in the presence of others so that you cultivate an inner dignity. People then see that you are carrying something special in your life. Offering respect to others, you will find that they return that respect.

Afterword

As we come to the end of this book, it is important to say something about the power of these qualities. We have worked with these transforming qualities now for many years and know that they are not 'just nice ideas'. They have practically and profoundly changed our lives and those of our colleagues in many ways.

The Controls and Directives promote total health and wellbeing of mind, body, and spirit. They also give energy, vitality and strength to those who practise them regularly. Because of the selfless energy imparted by these qualities you will find that your whole approach to life will move from local to global concerns. In short, these Controls and Directives help to affirm your responsibility towards humanity.

We have grouped the qualities into eight sections as shown overleaf. If you practise the Controls or Directives in the groups as shown, you will find that you can focus their effects into particular areas of your life.

The 12 Controls

The Controls	Benefits
Non-violence	Stabilises the body and mind
Truthfulness	
Not stealing	**Body area – adrenals**
Non-attachment	Learning to be untouched by life
Humility	**Body area – abdomen**
Non-possessiveness	**duodenum, small intestine**
Respect for principles	Creates energy for transformation
Living the highest	**Body area – liver**
Silence	**mid-spine, gall bladder**
Steadiness	Creates determination
Patience	
Courage	**Body area – colon, heart**

The 12 Directives

The Directives	Benefits
External purity	Cleanses the body and mind
Internal purity	Clears the vision
Singing power words	**Body area – endocrine and respiratory system**
Creative discipline	Gives strength, appreciation of life
Making life sacred	**Body area – heart**
Faith	**cardiac plexus, eyes**
Hospitality	Creates still and silent knowing
Silent gratitude	Connection with nature
	Body area – master glands –
Power of walking	**pituitary, pineal and thyroid**
Living the highest	Brings vision and purpose to life
Contentment	
Respect for that	**Body area – balances left/right**
which teaches us	**activity of brain**

About the authors

As a scientist, philosopher, author and visionary, Dr Mansukh Patel is one of the most dynamic and innovative teachers of self-development today. His unique approach to life combines a perfect blend of Eastern and Western cultures giving him a unique ability to relate to people at a very human level. His education began in Kenya at an early age with a programme of intensive training in self-awareness and culminated in a scientific career in bio-chemistry and cancer toxicology in the UK.

His fresh and vibrant approach to self-development has an appeal and relevance to all those who are looking for relief from the stresses of modern living and seeking to discover their true potential. Dr Patel is a best-selling author of many books and the subject of numerous TV documentaries including an award-winning 19-part TV commentary on the Bhagavad Gita.